MAN
VERSUS
MOUNTAIN

MOUNT
EVEREST

Bonnie
Hinman

PURPLE TOAD
PUBLISHING

P.O. Box 631
Kennett Square, Pennsylvania 19348
www.purpletoadpublishing.com

MAN
VERSUS
MOUNTAIN

K2 in Kashmir

Kilimanjaro

Mount Everest

Mount Fuji

Mount Olympus

Printing   1   2   3   4   5   6   7   8   9

Publisher's Cataloging-in-Publication Data
Hinman, Bonnie
 Mount Everest / Bonnie Hinman
     p. cm. – (Man versus mountain)
 Includes bibliographic references and index.
 ISBN: 978-1-62469-002-0 (library bound)
1. Everest, Mount (China and Nepal)--Juvenile literature.   I. Title.
DS495.8.E9 H56 2013
915.496—dc23
                                            2012955644

eBook ISBN: 978-1-62469-013-6

Printed by Lake Book Manufacturing, Chicago, IL

CONTENTS

CHAPTER 1

A Few More

WHACKS

Sir Edmund Hillary climbed across a rock slab and dropped into a tiny snow hollow. The bitter wind had blown ice crystals into his eyes, halfway blinding him. He should have known better than to remove his goggles while climbing a mountain over 29,000 feet (8,850 meters) high. His vision remained blurry even after he put his goggles back on. His climbing partner, Sherpa Tenzing Norgay, followed Hillary over the slab and into the hollow.

The rocks above them created a vertical bluff, or cliff, directly in their path to the summit. Hillary doubted that he and Norgay had enough strength at this altitude to climb straight up the rock face.

Hillary studied the bluff carefully to see if there might be a way around it. Not only could he not find an easy route, he couldn't find any route at all. There wasn't much time to waste. The men had only about four hours of oxygen left in their tanks. More would be

On a rare clear day Mount Everest can be seen jutting high above the other mountains.

Sir Edmund Hillary (left) and Sherpa Tenzing Norgay are wearing their snow goggles. Eye protection is vital for climbers high up on Everest because the reflection of the sun on the snow can temporarily blind a person.

needed to climb to the summit and back down to Camp IX, where they had a small reserve supply of oxygen. They both knew that to reach the summit any later than noon was to risk disaster. Storms often developed in the afternoons, which could trap them on the mountainside.

Hillary and Norgay were experienced and careful mountain climbers. There were probably few other people in the world who wanted to reach the summit of Mount Everest as much as they did. They knew they needed to turn around and head back down the mountain if they weren't standing on the summit by noon or shortly after.

Attached to the steep east face of Mount Everest was a large snow and ice-covered cornice. Cornices look like large snowdrifts that a person might see in a ditch along a road. They are deceptively dangerous. Made of snow that has blown and hardened into ice over a period of days or weeks, cornices eventually become unbalanced and tear away from the rock face of the mountain. They can tumble down the mountainside in great icy chunks.

Hillary saw a large crack between the cornice and the rock to which it was attached. A person could fit into this vertical crack—but the crack itself was proof that the cornice was already coming loose from the mountainside. The cornice looked hard and solid, but there was no way to be sure. It was a risk, but he was willing to take it. Hillary decided to climb up through the crack to the top of the bluff.

Norgay provided a belay by wrapping rope around his ice ax, which was imbedded in the ice. The rope was also attached to Hillary. Norgay steadied the rope. If Hillary fell, Norgay could haul him up using the rope. It was far from a foolproof plan, but Hillary knew he could count on his partner.

Hillary climbed into the crack and faced the mountainside. He saw some possible handholds in the rock. He grabbed the rock and jammed one of his spiked boots into the ice. The cornice held. Hillary wrote later that he was in constant fear that the cornice would peel away, taking him with it. He continued: "But slowly I forced my way up— wriggling and jambing and using every little hold. . . . I was reaching over the top of the rock and pulling myself to safety. The rope came tight—its forty feet had been barely enough."[1]

After a few moments' rest, Hillary signaled to Norgay to follow him. When both were on the rock ledge, they stared at the snowy ridge that stretched before them. The summit of Mount Everest was lost from view behind the ridge's curves. The pair stood up and began what they hoped would be the last set of steps they would have to cut into the icy snow.

Cutting steps with an ice ax is hard work, and at this altitude it was exhausting. Hillary and Norgay had no other choice if they hoped to reach the summit, but each time they rounded a curve of the ridge, another curve would appear. Hillary worried that the summit of Mount

Tenzing Norgay stands atop Mount Everest holding his ice axe above his head with flags flying. Norgay had wrapped four flags around his ice axe before the climb. The flags represented the United Nations: Britain, Nepal, and India.

Everest would be the crest or top of a cornice. If that were the case, all their work and preparation to reach the summit would disappear in disaster.

As Hillary rounded yet another curve of the ridge, he saw that it dropped away. He later wrote, "Out in the distance I could see the pastel shades and fleecy clouds of the highlands of Tibet."[2] He had reached the summit and now had only to determine if its top was a cornice.

"Peering from side to side and thrusting with my ice ax," he wrote, "I tried to discover a possible cornice, but everything seemed solid and firm. I waved Tenzing up to me. A few more whacks of the ice ax, a few very weary steps, and we were on the summit of Everest."[3]

At 11:30 a.m. on May 29, 1953, Sir Edmund Hillary and his Sherpa, Tenzing Norgay, became the first humans to reach the summit of Mount Everest and live to tell the story.

Facts About Mount Everest

Mount Everest, in the central Himalaya mountain range, is on the border between Nepal and Tibet in Central Asia. The highest place on earth, it is one of the famous Seven Summits—the highest peaks on each of the seven continents. Many Everest expeditions begin in Kathmandu, the capital city of Nepal. However, the staging area for the northern route is Lhasa, the capital of Tibet. Namche Bazaar is the last major town on the way to Everest Base Camp.

Location: longitude 86 55'40' E; latitude 270 45'N and 280 0'N

Names:

English: Mount Everest, after Welsh explorer and surveyor Sir George Everest

Nepali: Sagarmatha ("Goddess of the Sky")

Tibetan: Chomolungma ("Mother Goddess of the Universe")

Height: 29,035 feet (8,850 meters)

Climbing difficulty: While Everest is not as technically difficult as some other of the Seven Summits, altitude and weather conditions make it one of the most difficult—and deadly—climbs in the world. Improved equipment since the year 2000 has drastically improved the survival rate.

Number of climbers who have attempted to reach the summit: More than 3,200

Estimated number of climbers who have succeeded in reaching the summit: Between 600 and 700

Fatalities: About 233

Edmund Hillary, who was born on July 20, 1919, was a beekeeper in his native New Zealand. Beekeeping had a busy season, but during the off season Hillary climbed mountains all across New Zealand. By the time he reached the summit of Everest in 1953, he was an experienced climber.

The week that Hillary and Norgay reached Everest's summit was also the week of the coronation of Queen Elizabeth in England. This event became connected to the successful summit bid and drew more attention to Hillary than he ever expected. Later, Hillary was knighted by the new queen. His official name thereafter was Sir Edmund Hillary.

After the excitement over the summit expedition subsided, Hillary continued to climb. But most of his time was taken up with a new adventure. He devoted the rest of his life to providing schools and hospitals for the mountain people of Nepal. Later, he served as New Zealand High Commissioner to India.

Hillary died on January 11, 2008, and received a New Zealand state funeral. He had three children. The youngest, Belinda, died in a plane crash with her mother, Louise, in 1975. His other children, Sarah and Peter, have carried on his work in the Himalaya. Hillary's second wife, June, survived him.

Sir Edmund Hillary began climbing mountains as a young boy, reaching his first summit in 1939.

Tenzing Norgay had worked in the Himalaya mountains for almost twenty years before he summited Mount Everest on May 29, 1953. He didn't know his exact birthday but thought it was in late May in the Year of the Rabbit, which was 1915 in the Tibetan Calendar.

Norgay said he was born in Nepal, although some biographers think he was born in Tibet and later moved to Nepal. He spent much of his young adult life in India. He said that he was both Indian and Nepalese.

Although he could neither read nor write, Norgay spoke several languages. He climbed Everest several times with Swiss expeditions. He worked as a porter at first but gradually gained a reputation as an excellent guide and climber. The expedition with Hillary in 1953 was the seventh time Norgay had attempted to summit Everest.

Hillary and Norgay did not know one another before they partnered in 1953. During the weeks of acclimatization on Everest, Hillary saw Norgay's dedication to the climb. When Hillary slipped into a crevasse, Norgay saved his life, and Hillary asked him to be his partner.

Out of loyalty to and respect for one another, they refused to say who had stepped on top of Everest first. After Norgay's death in 1986, Hillary admitted that he had been first, but the pair always viewed it as a joint accomplishment.

In his later years, Norgay became director of field training for the Himalayan Mountaineering Institute in Darjeeling, India. He raised several children and was proud that the fame he earned on Everest allowed him to send them to good schools.

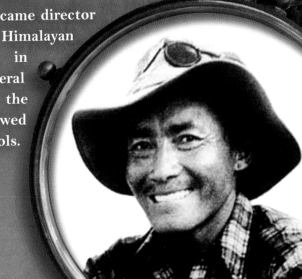

Tenzing Norgay and Sir Edmund Hillary remained friends and stayed in touch after their famous climb.

CHAPTER 2
Race to the
TOP

Sir Edmund Hillary and Tenzing Norgay's successful ascent to the top of Mount Everest was far from anyone's first attempt. People have been climbing mountains since ancient times. Climbing as a sport or pastime first took place in the mid-1800s in England and Europe. The Alpine Club, which was likely the first mountain climbing club, was founded in London in 1857.

The slopes and cliffs of England provided a training ground for mountaineers. Climbers often moved on to the more challenging heights of the Alps in Europe. In the late 1800s, they began to explore mountain ranges around the world. They climbed the Caucasus Mountains and several peaks in North America, including Pikes Peak, the Andes Mountains in Ecuador and Bolivia, and the mountains of Tierra del Fuego in South America.

In the early twentieth century, mountain climbers turned their eyes toward the Himalaya, the huge mountain range that splits Central Asia. Its tall peaks

Lucy Walker was a mountain climber in the Alps when women were not welcome. She made 98 ascents of various mountains in the mid-1800s. In this 1865 engraving, she is shown standing by the door in the background. This was not drawn from life so the fact that Walker was included with other famous mountain climbers shows the respect she gained.

were a place of mystery for many. The two countries on either side of the Himalaya, Nepal on the south and Tibet on the north, had closed borders. Political and religious issues kept these borders closed for years at a time. On the rare occasions when the borders were opened, there was strict control over climbing expeditions to Everest or any of the other nearby peaks.

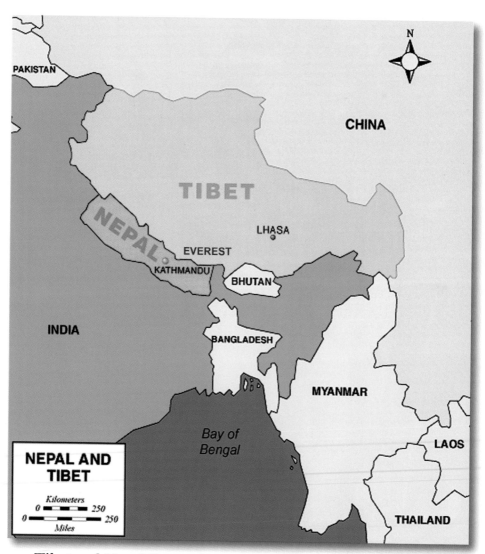

Tibet and Nepal lie north of India and are both landlocked.

Sir George Everest endured many hardships during his time as surveyor general of India and was often ill. When he retired, friends didn't expect him to survive long. He surprised everyone by living many years back home in Great Britain. Some historians think Everest may never have seen in person the mountain that was named after him.

Mount Everest was named after George Everest, surveyor-general of India. Everest had been in charge of a mapping survey of India and the Himalaya region. Surveyors measured mountains from a considerable distance away from the actual mountains themselves. They assigned each mountain a number, and Mount Everest was identified as number XV. After Everest retired from his post in 1843, Andrew Waugh took over as surveyor-general. Everest left instructions for Waugh to find out the local name for the mountain, but Waugh claimed that he and his crew could not discover any. Therefore, they named the mountain after their former boss. Everest was not pleased that his name would be used for the tallest mountain in the world.[1]

Despite the surveyors' inability to discover them, there were local names for number XV. In Tibet, Everest is called Chomolungma, which translates to "Goddess of the Universe." In Nepal, the mountain is called

Sagarmatha, which is said to mean either "Goddess of the Sky" or "Forehead of the Sky."[2]

English mountaineers planned expeditions to Everest in the early 1900s. They explored the areas around Everest to see if a climb to the summit would be possible. The first attempt to reach the summit was planned for 1916. World War I (1914–1918) broke out before then, and the plans were abandoned.

It wasn't until 1921 that the British scouted the Everest region again. In 1922 another expedition took climbers to a record height of 27,300 feet (8,320 meters). This team used an early form of oxygen tanks to help them breathe more easily at the high altitudes.

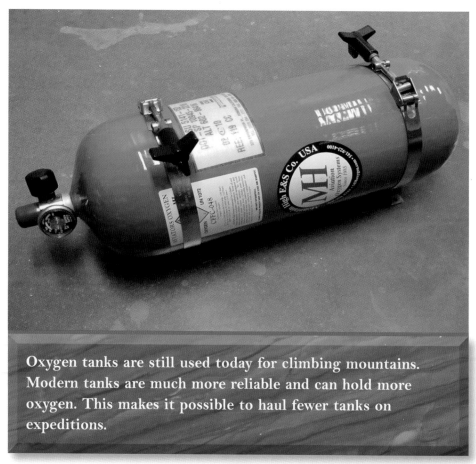

Oxygen tanks are still used today for climbing mountains. Modern tanks are much more reliable and can hold more oxygen. This makes it possible to haul fewer tanks on expeditions.

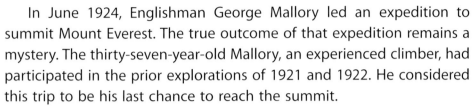

In June 1924, Englishman George Mallory led an expedition to summit Mount Everest. The true outcome of that expedition remains a mystery. The thirty-seven-year-old Mallory, an experienced climber, had participated in the prior explorations of 1921 and 1922. He considered this trip to be his last chance to reach the summit.

It was decided that two pairs of chosen climbers would attempt to reach the summit. All the other expedition members would serve as support. The first pair turned back before reaching the top because of trouble with their oxygen tanks. The second team, George Mallory and Andrew Irvine, set off in good weather from a base camp on Everest on June 8, 1924. Irvine was much less experienced and younger at twenty-two, but he was strong and knew a lot about the oxygen tanks they used.

Without the modern communication equipment that is used today, there was little way to know how the ascent was going. Occasionally, climbers high on the mountain could be seen from down below, but most of the time clouds or rocky cliffs blocked the view. A fellow climber, Noel Odell, was sure that he saw Mallory and Irvine climbing slowly upward high up on the ridge. But almost as soon as he saw them, clouds moved over the summit and hid the climbers from view. This was the last time that Mallory and Irvine were seen alive.[3]

Mallory and Irvine never returned to camp. Other climbers looked for them over the next couple of days, but the weather worsened as the monsoon season moved into the Himalaya.

Mystery surrounded their disappearance. Had they reached the summit and started back, or had something terrible happened? When Odell saw Mallory and Irvine on the mountain, it seemed as if they were still climbing. It was late to be ascending, but Odell thought it possible.

There was a brief snowstorm on the mountain that day, so they might have become lost in the storm and died of exposure. Perhaps they had fallen to their death. In the end, the main question remaining today is whether or not they died before or after reaching the summit.

Andrew Irving (far left) and George Mallory, standing next to his friend, are photographed with the rest of their nine-member expedition in 1924. The pair would perish on Everest soon after this photo was taken.

Heavy snow, as well as melting and shifting glaciers, kept everyone off the mountain until fall. The search resumed—the whereabouts of Mallory and Irvine remained a mystery for seventy-five years.

Finally, Mallory's frozen body was found in 1999. Researchers still could not tell whether Mallory and Irvine had reached the summit, but they were able to provide answers to other questions. It was apparent from the position of the body that Mallory had died after a fall. He had sustained several broken bones and a head injury. The camera that Mallory carried was not found—and neither was Irvine's body. Today, climbers continue to look for the missing camera. It may hold proof of whether or not the pair reached the summit.

In the years following the disastrous 1924 expedition, several climbing groups from various countries attempted to reach the summit. They improved climbing techniques and learned much more about high-altitude climbing with bottled oxygen, but they did not reach the top of Mount Everest.

World War II (1939–1945) stopped all climbing efforts. It wasn't until the 1950s that climbers set their sights on Mount Everest again.

Great Britain colonized India in the mid to late 1700s. By the early 1800s, the English needed a map to keep track of their land and people. Therefore, in 1802, the Great Trigonometric Survey commenced in India. The area surveyed and mapped was called the Great Arc, a huge amount of land spanning from the tip of India to the Himalaya.

Difficulties arose when British surveyors reached the far western part of the arc. Nepal and Tibet were not allowing foreigners into their lands. It was almost impossible to get close enough to use the usual surveying instruments.

The determined surveyors sometimes sneaked across borders to measure mountains and other landforms. With so many obstacles to overcome, the survey was not completed until 1842. It would be several years before the results were declared official.

In 1852, the surveyors came to the conclusion that the mountain now known as Mount Everest was 29,002 feet (8,842 meters) high. This made it the highest location on earth. Some survey officials thought the measurement was too high and questioned the methods used. Most of the calculations had been made from a distance. The height wasn't even publicly announced until 1856.

In fact, the height the survey reported was amazingly close to the altitude calculated in 1999: 29,029 feet (8,848 meters).[4]

The Great Theodolite was a huge device used to measure angles during the Great Trigonometric Survey.

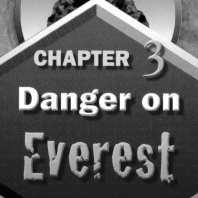

CHAPTER 3
Danger on
Everest

Climbing Mount Everest is similar to climbing other large mountains, but there are important differences that climbers need to know before attempting this expedition.

The weather on Everest can be extreme. Generally, it is only possible to climb during spring, which lasts just a few weeks in April and May. Even then, temperatures can drop to below minus 40 degrees Fahrenheit (minus 40 degrees Celsius). Almost daily in the afternoons, fierce storms can blow up, bringing icy winds and blinding snowstorms. On Everest, more people die of exposure than by falling.

Another danger to climbers is altitude sickness. It can affect people at any altitude that is much higher than what they are used to. It is common for those who climb higher than 8,000 feet (2,500 meters), or for those who climb more than 1640 feet (500 meters) in elevation per day to feel its effects.[1]

Lightweight aluminum ladders are often used to bridge crevasses that must be crossed on the way up Everest. This climber is wearing crampons on his boots and is anchored to a safety rope with a hook.

Altitude sickness usually begins with a headache that intensifies at higher elevations. Commonly, the headache will disappear if a climber remains at the same altitude for a period of time or descends the mountain. Symptoms can rapidly grow worse and include nausea, vomiting, muscle weakness, loss of appetite, and difficulty sleeping. Those who suffer from this sickness may do irrational things. They may throw off vital equipment or simply step off the edge of the mountain. They may forget to eat or drink. These symptoms may increase until a climber suffers from pulmonary edema, which is water in the lungs, and cerebral edema, which is water in the brain and can cause a coma.[2] The fastest cure for altitude sickness is a quick descent to a lower altitude and an increase in the person's oxygen supply.

Altitude sickness is the result of thinner air at high elevations. Earth's atmosphere is like an ocean of air. At sea level, the air is compressed by all the air above it. Air pressure gradually decreases the higher you go. With less pressure, the molecules in the air spread out. On top of Mount Everest, the air pressure is about one-third of what it would be at sea level. Therefore, there is one-third the amount of air—and the oxygen molecules in the air—in the same amount of space. This is true inside the body as well. With each breath, climbers inhale much less oxygen than it takes for the body to work efficiently.[3] To make up for the lack of oxygen at these heights, climbers will carry tanks of compressed oxygen.

Humans can adapt to lower pressure over time, and some have even climbed Everest without the aid of oxygen tanks, but this is uncommon. All climbers must first acclimate themselves to the thin air at such great heights. They set up camps near the bottom of Everest and live there for a few days or weeks. They gradually climb the mountain, setting up campsites at higher and higher elevations. Often they will climb during the day and return to a lower camp to sleep.

This routine continues until they reach about 26,000 feet (8,000 m). Above that is the Death Zone, an area where a human's physical and mental condition will deteriorate rapidly. It is not possible to acclimate at that altitude, so climbers ascend to the summit and immediately return to safer elevations. Staying at the summit for longer than 30 minutes is not recommended.[4]

The human body makes more red blood cells during these acclimatizing stays. More red blood cells carry more oxygen, making it easier to tolerate higher altitudes. For unknown reasons, some people seem to be able to acclimatize more quickly and completely than others. This ability to adapt to the altitude is one of the most important criteria for a successful climb, and it cannot be determined by anything other than experience.

The Sherpa, for example, make their homes high in the mountains. They are farmers, sheep herders, and mountain guides or porters. They are much less likely to get altitude sickness and are able to perform

This is a Sherpa family who lives high in the Himalayan Mountains. The Sherpa people are friendly and welcome visitors to their high-altitude villages.

physical labor with ease thousands of feet high in the Himalaya. While it is not fully understood why they have these advantages at high altitudes, it is known that their hearts and lungs have developed ways to compensate for the thinner air.

The Sherpa can earn higher wages on mountain climbing expeditions than they can by farming or raising animals. Other mountain people may work as porters, carrying gear or guiding pack-carrying yaks, but the high-altitude work is almost always done by the Sherpa. The most experienced Sherpa may become sirdars, or foreman of the Sherpa, and are usually paid more.

Other dangers on Everest are much less predictable than altitude sickness. Avalanches have killed many more Everest climbers than altitude sickness has. Small movements of the glaciers surrounding Everest may shift snow, and in an instant an avalanche may rumble down the mountain. Climbers who are on the edge of the snowfield may be tossed aside and live. Those in its direct path will be buried. An experienced guide might be able to tell if the conditions are right for an avalanche, but he or she cannot predict when, or even if, one will happen.

An 1803 painting by Phillip James de Loutherbourg, *Avalanche in the Alps*, shows the destruction of an avalanche.

The great depth of this crevasse can be measured against the size of the climbers in the background. The layers of snow and ice are clear in the sides of the giant crack.

Climbers also have to be wary of crevasses, deep cracks in the ice and rocks. The glaciers that cover Everest and the surrounding mountains are always moving. This movement can create large crevasses or cover existing ones. Large ones are easy to see, but smaller ones may be covered with snow and are easy to step into.

The easiest way to get across crevasses is by walking across snow or ice that has built up into a bridge that spans the gap. A climber can't always tell how strong a snow bridge is. He or she must proceed cautiously, and only when roped securely to a solid rock or a climbing

This climber is crossing a crevasse on a snow bridge. Tracks show that the snow bridge has been successfully crossed already, but the climber is still hooked to a safety rope.

partner. Aluminum ladders have been anchored across some of the large crevasses on Everest. Climbers can crawl across these ladders, which may bridge gaps of 15 to 20 feet (4 to 6 meters).

Ropes play an important role in making mountain climbing safer than it would be otherwise. On Everest, fixed ropes are put in place each year at the beginning of the season. They are firmly attached to rock or ice with screws. Climbers can clip onto the ropes using ascenders, gadgets that allow the rope to pass through only one way. This limits the distance a climber can fall if he or she slips.

Although modern equipment such as ascenders, more efficient oxygen tanks, and portable satellite phones have made it safer to climb Everest than before, climbers still trudge up a treacherous path to the summit. Mallory was once asked why he wanted to climb Everest. His famous answer was, "Because it's there."[5]

Stories of the Abominable Snowman are some of the most persistent legends to come out of the Himalaya. Often called a Yeti, this creature is reported to look part human and part animal, is very tall, and covered with fur or hair. It has been said that the Yeti has a strong odor that smells like garlic. It can be aggressive or gentle, depending on the tale.

Dozens of climbers and locals have claimed to see Yeti footprints. More than a few people have said they came face to face with it. Some sightings are fictional, but even respected scholars have undertaken searches for the Yeti. Sir Edmund Hillary led one such expedition in 1960. Clear photographs do not exist—or at least not ones whose owners can prove that the photos are real.

Another popular legend is that of Shangri-La, which is supposed to be a hidden mystical place of beauty and harmony. The people of this hidden valley are permanently happy. This legend began with James Hilton's novel *Lost Horizon,* which was published in 1933. The story takes place in an isolated valley surrounded by mountains. Later, two movies were based on the novel. Fans of the book and movies thought that Hilton had based his book on an actual place somewhere in the Himalaya. Hilton had traveled the Himalaya, but there is no proof that he used any real place to represent Shangri-La. The search for Shangri-La continues today.

This drawing of the Yeti shows his fierce attitude and size.

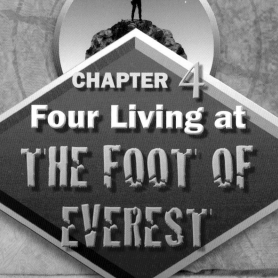

Four Living at THE FOOT OF EVEREST

Mount Everest sits squarely on the border between Nepal and Tibet. Both are ancient countries with rich and varied cultures and histories. While they have many things in common, they are still quite different.

Tibet's earliest residents lived on the Tibetan Plateau as many as 21,000 years ago. By 100 BCE, there were several independent kingdoms in Tibet. Songtsen Gampo became king around 617 CE. During his reign, he unified Tibet. Following his time on the throne, Tibet was ruled by many kings who expanded Tibetan territories into an empire. In the ninth century, a civil war over who would be the next king caused the empire to split apart.[1]

Tibet has often been under the rule of China. Mongol rulers also eyed Tibet, but distance and terrain interfered with their plans. Sometimes there would be decades of peaceful rule with Tibetans largely in control.

The snow leopard makes its home in Central Asia's mountainous regions including those in Tibet and Nepal. It is an endangered species with an estimated 4,000 to 5,000 leopards remaining in and around the Himalayan Mountains. The snow leopard has never been known to kill humans, but does prey on domestic animals. This situation causes friction with farmers who want to protect their livestock.

Buddhism arrived in Tibet from India in the seventh century. This belief system has deeply influenced Tibet's culture and history. The Dalai Lama is the spiritual leader of Buddhists.

The fourteenth Dalai Lama took over in 1950, right after China invaded Eastern Tibet. Political unrest plagued Tibet until the Dalai Lama was forced to flee the country in 1959. He continues to have a great deal of influence in Tibetan affairs, and since 1963 has worked to establish Tibet as an independent democracy. Fifty years later, Tibet remained an autonomous region of China, with the Tibetan government operating in exile from Dharamsala, India.[2]

Tibetans maintain an unending quest to bring the Dalai Lama back to Tibet to lead their country. The Chinese insist that Tibet is now and always has been a part of China. Violent and nonviolent protests against China are common.[3]

Life in Tibet is uncertain at best, but the Tibetan people are friendly and welcoming. Permits to climb Mount Everest and other mountains are a welcome source of income to the Chinese, so most of the time the borders are open.

Tibet's neighbor to the south, Nepal, is more diverse than Tibet in many ways. Different ethnic groups and religions coexist with very little friction. Like Tibetans, the Nepalese are friendly and welcoming. Geography and weather are two elements that greatly affect the life of the Nepalese. Lifestyles vary depending on the region.

The lowlands in southern Nepal are called the Terai. This region has warm winters and hot, wet summers. The altitude ranges from sea level at the border with India to as high as 1,640 feet (500 meters), where the plain turns into low foothills. The fertile land provides food for most of Nepal.

The hill region is located in the middle of Nepal. It has a more temperate climate, with cool winters and warm, wet summers. The capital city of Nepal, Kathmandu, is located here. Kathmandu Valley has been home to settlers since the seventh century BCE. Throughout the centuries, it has attracted people from all over Nepal, Tibet, and India.

Macaque monkeys are considered holy in much of Asia. Here they are being fed on the streets of Kathmandu, Nepal.

Kathmandu sits in one of the most earthquake-prone regions in the world. As the edges of Earth's tectonic plates push against one another, they raise mountains and cause earthquakes. The Himalaya were raised like this thousands of years ago, and they continue to grow up to 1 centimeter per year.[4] Not only is Kathmandu close to this fault line, it is also on soft soil, which increases the danger posed by earthquakes. In 1934, an earthquake destroyed much of the city. The remaining parts of the old city have narrow alleyways lined with tiny shops, bazaars, temples, and stupas.

In the past, Kathmandu was the only place accessible to mountain climbers who planned to tackle Mount Everest. They arrived, hired porters, and tramped for weeks carrying supplies to their base camp. Today, supplying Everest expeditions is much easier. There are more roads and airstrips that can accommodate planes bringing supplies for the climbers.

The high-altitude or alpine zone of Nepal has cold winters and cool summers. This is the home of the Sherpa and other hardy people who are mostly farmers or yak herders. The shaggy-haired yak is all-important to both Nepal and Tibet. With their large lungs and hearts, yaks are able to live high on the mountainsides. Yaks are used for their milk, meat, and fiber and as beasts of burden. Their dung is used for fuel, especially on the Tibetan Plateau, which is largely treeless.

Nepal's geography has also influenced its history. In ancient days it was a resting place for travelers as they passed through the Himalaya to trade in Kathmandu or to continue to India. Like Tibet, the borders of Nepal have been closed to foreigners from time to time. There have been long periods of peaceful rule by kings and times of squabbling among independent states.

Caste and social status are important in Nepal. In a caste system, all people are born into a social level that indicates their importance and acceptance in society. They remain in that caste for life. Members of each caste have certain rights and responsibilities. For example, members of the lowest caste are not permitted to enter the homes of those from the highest caste. Marriage between castes is forbidden.

Nepal suffered greatly during a civil war that lasted from 1996 to 2006. Members of the Chinese Communist Political Party, also called Maoists, fought against the Nepalese government to bring reforms to Nepal. The Maoists called the uprising The People's War. Compromises ended the conflict, and Nepal became an uneasy democracy.[5]

The politics of Nepal and Tibet have often influenced the conquest of Mount Everest. Both the northern route via Tibet and the southern route via Nepal have advantages and disadvantages. Mallory and Irving climbed the northern route because the borders of Nepal were closed at the time. Hillary and Norgay climbed the southern route because the borders of Tibet were closed when they planned their trip.

The conquest of Everest might have occurred differently had the Tibetan and Nepali borders always been open.

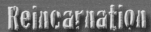

Buddhists believe that when a person dies, his or her spirit is reborn into a new body as a baby. This process is called reincarnation. The person has no memories of the previous life or body although some people claim to be able to rouse those memories in themselves and others.

Into what body or situation a person is reborn depends on his or her behavior. A person who lives an honorable life and adheres to Buddhist beliefs may be reborn as a more important or richer person. A person who did not live by Buddhist beliefs might be reborn as an insect. The cycle of birth, death, and rebirth continues until a person reaches perfection, or nirvana.

Reincarnation plays a role in the selection of a new Dalai Lama when the old one dies. Buddhist leaders searching for a new Dalai Lama look for a young boy who is the reincarnation of the past Dalai Lama. The leaders have several ways of telling who this is. The location of the boy may come to one of them in a dream or vision. When the boy is presented with a group of items, the leaders watch to see if the boy picks up any items that belonged to the previous Dalai Lama. The chosen boy is taken from his home, sometimes with his family, to be educated and trained. Many years go by after a Dalai Lama dies before the new one is found and made ready for his important duties.

The Dalai Lama

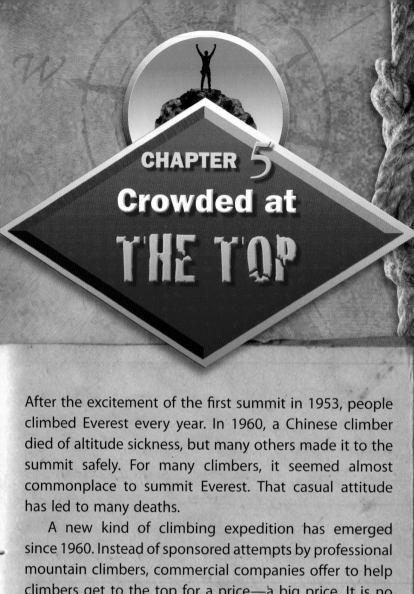

CHAPTER 5
Crowded at
THE TOP

After the excitement of the first summit in 1953, people climbed Everest every year. In 1960, a Chinese climber died of altitude sickness, but many others made it to the summit safely. For many climbers, it seemed almost commonplace to summit Everest. That casual attitude has led to many deaths.

A new kind of climbing expedition has emerged since 1960. Instead of sponsored attempts by professional mountain climbers, commercial companies offer to help climbers get to the top for a price—a big price. It is no longer necessary to be a professional or even an experienced climber. For those who have the money, commercial companies will arrange all the details of the expedition and provide a level of safety for them. In 2012, a permit to climb Everest was about $10,000. A company could be hired for anywhere between $10,000 and $35,000.[1]

The number of climbers on Everest has increased dramatically from the early years. Almost all climbers now join commercial expeditions, which are led by professional guides.

The official permit to climb Mount Everest.

Climbers still needed to be physically fit and have some climbing experience, but there were commercial companies that would take tourists without either. This commercialization has made Everest extremely crowded. In 1996, the deadliest year on Everest, fifteen climbers met their deaths. Eight of them died on May 10–11 during a summit attempt. Two died most likely from falls, the other six from exposure.

There were many delays on May 10 before the window of clear weather opened up for the race to the summit. There were so many climbers ready to go, they had to wait in line for their turn to ascend the fixed ropes on some of the steep rock cliffs. These bottlenecks kept the climbers in the Death Zone for a dangerously long time.[2]

That afternoon, the weather turned sharply worse, bringing a blizzard. It was generally agreed among guides that 2:00 p.m. was the latest to reach the summit if a climber was to get back to safety before stormy weather hit. If reaching the top of Everest was not possible by 2:00 p.m., climbers were to stop and turn back. None of the six who died of exposure followed that rule.

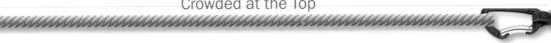

Jon Krakauer, a survivor of that deadly climb, wrote a popular book about the disaster. In *Into Thin Air*, he concludes that commercial guides had allowed unqualified climbers to attempt the climb, and the use of bottled oxygen gave them a false sense of security. He also believes that competition among expedition companies added pressure to reach the summit in spite of growing danger. Three of the commercial guides were among the dead.[3]

Another especially deadly year for climbers was 2006. Eleven climbers lost their lives during the April–May climbing season. Two particular stories stand out: one of a tragic death and the other of a miraculous survival.

Thirty-four-year-old David Sharp of the United Kingdom was not part of an official expedition. He had obtained his permit through a commercial expedition company. To save money, Sharp traveled solo—without a guide or other support staff. If solo climbers get into trouble during their climb, there is nobody who is officially responsible for helping him or her.

Sharp had reached the summit on May 14 but ran into trouble on his way back down. As he lay in a small rocky alcove, as many as forty other climbers passed him. Some thought he was dead, while others stopped to talk to him. Some climbers and Sherpa tried to help him, but he couldn't walk or even stand. Nobody seemed to realize that Sharp was a solo climber who had no one to help him. Sharp died of exposure and frostbite within sight of the main trail.[4]

His death stirred a great controversy about climbing ethics on Mount Everest. Should climbers have sacrificed their chance to reach the summit in order to rescue someone who might have died no matter what they did? Should those on their way down have done something more to save Sharp? Is it ever right to abandon someone to die alone on a mountaintop even if staying with him might endanger the rescuer?

With no easy answers, the controversy swirled around for days in the media. The subject was further complicated when another climber was miraculously rescued ten days later. New Zealander Lincoln Hall had successfully reached the summit on May 25 but began suffering on his way down from what was probably cerebral edema, an advanced form of altitude sickness.

The good-natured Hall became violent and delirious. The four Sherpa with him managed with a great struggle to get him partway down the mountain. At about 28,000 feet (8,500 meters) on the Northeast Ridge, still in the Death Zone, Hall collapsed. There was no rousing him. The Sherpa thought he was dead. They left him and climbed down to safety.

Hall wasn't dead and in fact survived the night. When climbing resumed in the morning, guide Dan Mazur approached what he thought was Hall's corpse. Suddenly, Hall opened his eyes and looked at Mazur. "I imagine you're surprised to see me here," said Hall.[5] *Shocked* was a better description of Mazur's reaction.

Mazur's team gave up their chance to reach the summit to nurse Hall until he could walk with some support. Sherpa guided him down to base camp and safety.

The 2012 spring climbing season brought more death and controversy. Ten people died in April and May, six of them on the weekend of May 19–20. Song Won Bin of South Korea died after a fall near the summit, which may have been caused by dizziness. The other five died of exhaustion, exposure, or altitude sickness.

Almost immediately, the media blamed overcrowding as the cause of the deaths. The bottlenecks existed on both the Tibetan and Nepali routes. According to unofficial numbers compiled by Alan Arnette, an expert climber who blogged day by day about the 2012 season, 946 climbers went up Everest from both sides. Of that number, 548 made it to the top and back down safely.[6]

Arnette relates that there were many other reasons for the high death count in 2012. The weather was ominous from early in the season. Snow that usually covered rocks on the mountain, which would limit rock fall danger, did not arrive at its usual time. Avalanches and huge ice blocks were waiting to tumble down the mountain. The usual

Climbers navigate an ice block the size of a small house.

southern route was changed because of these dangers. While the detour helped limit danger from rock falls, the route was longer and required more energy to finish.

A few expedition companies pulled out for the season. The window for good-climbing weather that normally appeared for eleven days or so in early to middle May didn't arrive as expected. That window shrank to about four days, creating crowds on the mountain when the first window appeared on May 18.

Some climbers, both experienced and inexperienced, took dangerous chances because they feared that they would miss their chance to summit. They ignored turnaround times and refused to follow the advice of the Sherpa who told them to descend immediately. Eberhard Schaaf, a sports doctor from Germany who had climbed Mount McKinley in Alaska, Kilimanjaro in Tanzania, and Aconcagua in Argentina, was one who ignored them. Losing track of time, he spent an hour in the Death Zone, and then had to wait two hours in a bottleneck for his turn to descend. Before he reached safety, Schaaf lost his eyesight, and then collapsed. His guides could not revive him.

In the village of Dughla, Nepal, a memorial stands as a testament to the more than 233 people who have died on Everest. The family of Eberhard Schaaf would add a memorial stone for him.

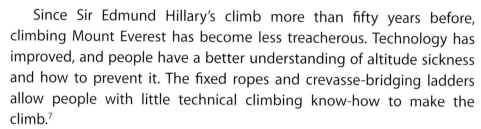

Since Sir Edmund Hillary's climb more than fifty years before, climbing Mount Everest has become less treacherous. Technology has improved, and people have a better understanding of altitude sickness and how to prevent it. The fixed ropes and crevasse-bridging ladders allow people with little technical climbing know-how to make the climb.[7]

Mount Everest is plagued with the aftermath of all this human activity. It is littered with discarded oxygen tanks, trash, and human waste. There have been efforts to clean up the garbage, but it has proved a dangerous task.

Left behind on the mountain are also as many as two hundred bodies. Most of the people who die in the Death Zone are left there. It is too dangerous to bring a body down from that height. Sherpa can sometimes carry down people who die below the Death Zone, but it is expensive. Why can't they be airlifted out? The air is too thin above 23,000 feet (7,000 meters) for helicopter blades to generate enough lift.[8]

Mount Everest is a dangerous place. Climber Alan Arnette said this about the deaths on Everest in 2012: "The dead died from their own ambitions, not from rocks or ice or falls. They died because they took a risk of being where humans are not designed to be; and they lost."[9]

Mount Everest, where man versus mountain goes on.

Despite harsh conditions and habitat destruction in the Himalaya, many animals flourish there. The Bengal tiger is protected and maintained in several national parks in Nepal. The tiger is a target for poachers, who sell its body parts for traditional medicines and clothing. Another protected animal is the shy snow leopard. It is believed that only a few hundred snow leopards remain in the high mountains.

There are also several species of deer, including the barking deer with its scream-like call. It is believed to be the oldest species of deer on earth. The tiny musk deer, which measures 20 inches (50 centimeters) at the shoulder, lives at high altitudes. It has been depleted by hunting for its musk gland.[10]

There are nine kinds of vultures in Nepal, and three of them are critically endangered. They died in great numbers after scavenging dead cows that had been treated with antibiotics. Some areas of Nepal have had great success by starting "vulture restaurants." These special feeding stations are stocked with uncontaminated meat for the hungry birds.[11]

In spite of their reputations as fierce hunters, Bengal tigers usually avoid humans.

Chapter One: A Few More Whacks

1. Sir Edmund Hillary, *High Adventure: The True Story of the First Ascent of Everest* (Oxford: Oxford University Press, 1955), p. 224.
2. Ibid., p. 226.
3. Ibid.

Chapter Two: Race to the Top

1. Richard Sale and George Rodway, *Everest and Conquest in the Himalaya: Science and Courage on the World's Highest Mountain* (Barnsley, South Yorkshire, UK: Pen & Sword Books Ltd, 2011), pp. 12–13.
2. Alexa Johnston, *Reaching the Summit: Sir Edmund Hillary's Life of Adventure* (New York: DK Publishing, Inc. 2005), p. 49.
3. Liesl Clark and Audrey Salkeld, "Lost on Everest: The Mystery of Mallory & Irvine '24," *PBS Online,* November 2000, http://www.pbs.org/wgbh/nova/everest/lost/mystery/
4. Sale and Rodway, p. 13.

Chapter Three: Danger on Everest

1. Altitude.org: "Altitude Sickness," http://www.altitude.org/altitude_sickness.php
2. Richard Sale and George Rodway, *Everest and Conquest in the Himalaya: Science and Courage on the World's Highest Mountain* (Barnsley, South Yorkshire, UK: Pen & Sword Books Ltd, 2011), pp. 101–103.
3. Ibid., p. 18.
4. Lukas Eberle, "Congestion in the Death Zone: The Story Behind Another Deadly Year on Everest," *Spiegel Online International,* October 5, 2012, http://www.spiegel.de/international/zeitgeist/mount-everest-records-deadliest-year-in-over-a-decade-a-859533.html
5. David Breashears, *High Exposure: An Enduring Passion for Everest and Unforgiving Places* (New York: Simon & Schuster, 1999), p. 121.

Chapter Four: Living at the Foot of Everest

1. Thomas Laird, *The Story of Tibet: Conversations With the Dalai Lama* (New York: Grove Press, 2006), p. 28.

2. Ibid., p. 303.
3. Ben Blanchard, "Teens Set Themselves on Fire, Take Tibet Burnings over 50," *Chicago Tribune,* August 27, 2012, http://articles.chicagotribune.com/2012-08-27/news/ sns-rt-us-china-tibetbre87r031-20120827_1_tibetans-burnings-himalayan-homeland
4. Krishna Pokharel, "Nepal's Big One: Myth or Reality?" *The Wall Street Journal,* September 21, 2011, http://blogs.wsj.com/indiarealtime/2011/09/21/ nepals-big-one-myth-or-reality/
5. Bradley Mayhew, Lindsay Brown, Trent Holden, *Lonely Planet Nepal* (London: Lonely Planet Publications Pty Ltd, 2012), pp. 314–318.

Chapter Five: Crowded at the Top

1. Lukas Eberle, "Congestion in the Death Zone: The Story Behind Another Deadly Year on Everest," *Spiegel Online International,* October 5, 2012, http://www.spiegel.de/international/zeitgeist/mount-everest-records-deadliest-year-in-over-a-decade-a-859533.html
2. Jon Krakauer, *Into Thin Air* (New York: Random House, Inc., 1997), pp. 175–178.
3. Ibid., pp. 272–274.
4. Lincoln Hall, *Dead Lucky: Life After Death on Mount Everest* (New York: Jeremy P. Tarcher/Penguin, 2007), pp. 262–264.
5. Ibid., p. 195.
6. Alan Arnette, "Everest 2012: Season Recap: A Study in Risk Management," Blog, May 30, 2012, http:www.alanarnette.com/blog/2012/05/30/ everest-2012-season-recap-a-study-in-risk-management/
7. Katherine Tarbox, "The Economics of Everest," *Time Moneyland,* http:// moneyland.time.com/2012/01/23/the-economics-of-everest/
8. Eberle.
9. Arnette.
10. Bradley Mayhew, Lindsay Brown, Trent Holden, *Lonely Planet Nepal* (London: Lonely Planet Publications Pty Ltd, 2012), p. 342.
11. Ibid., p. 344.

Books

Blanc, Katherine. *The Boy Who Conquered Everest: The Jordan Romero Story.* New York: Hay House, Inc., 2010.

Doyle, Bill H. *Everest.* San Francisco: Chronicle Books, 2011.

Graham, Ian. *You Wouldn't Want to Climb Mount Everest!: A Deadly Journey to the Top of the World.* New York: Franklin Watts, 2010.

McCollum, Sean. "Into the Death Zone," *Scholastic Scope,* February 14, 2011, Vol. 59, Issue 10.

Smith, Roland. *Peak.* Orlando: Harcourt, Inc., 2008.

Works Consulted

Alan Arnette. "Everest 2012: Season Recap: A Study in Risk Management." Blog, May 30, 2012, http://www.alanarnette.com/blog/2012/05/30/everest-2012-season-recap-a-study-in-risk-management/

Blanchard, Ben. "Teens Set Themselves on Fire, Take Tibet Burnings Over 50." *Chicago Tribune,* August 27, 2012. http://articles.chicagotribune.com/2012-08-27/news/sns-rt-us-china-tibetbre87r031-20120827_1_tibetans-burnings-himalayan-homeland

Boukreev, Anatoli, and G. Weston DeWalt. *The Climb: Tragic Ambitions on Everest.* New York: St. Martin's Press, 1997.

Breashears, David. *High Exposure: An Enduring Passion for Everest and Unforgiving Places.* New York: Simon & Schuster, 1999.

Clark, Liesl, and Audrey Salkeld. "Lost on Everest: The Mystery of Mallory & Irvine '24." *PBS Online,* November 2000. http://www.pbs.org/wgbh/nova/everest/lost/mystery/

Davis, Wade. *Into the Silence: The Great War, Mallory and the Conquest of Everest.* New York: Knopf, 2011.

Dickinson, Matt. *The Other Side of Everest.* Thorndike, Maine: Thorndike Press, 1999.

Eberle, Lukas. "Congestion in the Death Zone: The Story Behind Another Deadly Year on Everest." *Spiegel Online International,* October 5, 2012. http://www.spiegel.de/international/zeitgeist/mount-everest-records-deadliest-year-in-over-a-decade-a-859533.html

Hall, Lincoln. *Dead Lucky: Life After Death on Mount Everest.* New York: Jeremy P. Tarcher/Penguin, 2007.

Harrer, Heinrich. *Seven Years in Tibet.* New York: Tarcher/Putnam, 1953.

Hillary, Sir Edmund. *High Adventure: The True Story of the First Ascent of Everest.* Oxford: Oxford University Press, 1955.

Johnston, Alexa. *Reaching the Summit: Sir Edmund Hillary's Life of Adventure.* New York: DK Publishing, Inc., 2005.

Kashish. "Everest: Dying for the High." *Republica, The Week,* May 25, 2012. http://theweek.myrepublica.com/details.php?news_id=35506

Krakauer, Jon. *Into Thin Air.* New York: Random House, Inc., 1997.

Laird, Thomas. *The Story of Tibet: Conversations with the Dalai Lama.* New York: Grove Press, 2006.

Mayhew, Bradley, Lindsay Brown, Trent Holden. *Lonely Planet Nepal.* London: Lonely Planet Publications Pty Ltd, 2012.

Norgay, Jamling Tenzing, with Broughton Coburn. *Touching My Father's Soul.* San Francisco: HarperSanFrancisco, 2001.

Pokharel, Krishna. "Nepal's Big One: Myth or Reality?" *The Wall Street Journal,* September 21, 2011. http://blogs.wsj.com/indiarealtime/2011/09/21/nepals-big-one-myth-or-reality/

Powers, John. *A Concise Introduction to Tibetan Buddhism.* Ithaca, NY: Snow Lion Publications, 2008.

Reynolds, Kev. *Everest, A Trekker's Guide.* Milnthorpe, Cumbria, UK: Cicerone, 2011.

Roach, Gerry. *Why Everest: A Short History of the Pioneers.* Montrose, Colorado: Summit Sight, 2012.

Sale, Richard, and George Rodway. *Everest and Conquest in the Himalaya: Science and Courage on the World's Highest Mountain.* Barnsley, South Yorkshire, UK: Pen & Sword Books Ltd, 2011.

Schaffer, Grayson. "Take a Number." *Outside Magazine,* October 2012. http://www.outsideonline.com/outdoor-adventure/climbing/mountaineering/Everest-2012-take-a-number/.

Shortcuts Blog. "Mount Everest: The Ethical Dilemma Facing Climbers." http://www.guardian.co.uk/world/shortcuts/2012/may/28/mount-everest-ethical-dilemma/

Tarbox, Katherine. "The Economics of Everest." *Time Moneyline.* January 23, 2012. http://moneyland.time.com/2012/01/23/the-economics-of-everest/

On the Internet

Abominable Snowman
http://natgeotv.com/uk/abominable-snowman/facts

Altitude.org: Altitude Sickness
http://www.altitude.org/altitude_sickness.php

Geology for Kids! Himalayan Mountains
http://scienceforkids.kidipede.com/geology/platetectonics/himalayas.htm

Kids' Planet Animal Fact Sheets
http://www.kidsplanet.org/factsheets/map.html

PBS/NOVA: Everest
http://www.pbs.org/wgbh/nova/everest/

Preparing for Everest—6 Months Out
http://www.alanarnette.com/blog/2012/11/01/preparing-for-everest-6-minths-out/

Glossary

acclimate—To become adjusted to a certain climate or environment.

alcove—A small recess in a wall.

amateur—A person who engages in something for pleasure rather than money.

ascender—A mechanical device used in mountain climbing.

ascent—The act of climbing up.

autonomous—Region in Tibet that is self-governing but part of China.

belay—To secure by attaching to one end of a rope.

bottleneck—A place where a path or route narrows, slowing down the flow of traffic.

cornice—A mass of snow jutting out over a mountain ledge.

coronation—The act of crowning a king or queen.

deteriorate—To get worse.

ethics—A system or code of behaviors.

exile—Forced to live away from one's country.

expedition—Group that sets out on a trip for a specific purpose; or a trip for a specific purpose.

exposure—Being in harsh weather conditions without any protection.

fault line—A break or series of breaks in layers of rock that may cause earthquakes when they shift.

frostbite—Skin and tissue damage caused by exposure to intense cold.

glacier—A large mass of snow and ice that moves over land until it melts or breaks.

monsoon—A seasonal wind that blows in heavy rains over an area.

Sherpa—A member of a group in Tibet used as porters on mountain-climbing expeditions.

stupa—A dome-shaped Buddhist shrine.

summit—The highest point of a hill or mountain.

surveyor—One who performs a detailed measurement of land.

tectonic plates—Massive slabs of rock that float slowly over the surface of the earth, they may collide or one may slide under another and change into liquid rock.

terrain—The natural shape or condition of a piece of land.

treacherous—Posing danger.

About the

AUTHOR

Bonnie Hinman has had more than 30 children's books published, most of which have been nonfiction biography, geography, and science. She has been interested in mountains ever since taking a geology course in college. Yet, she prefers to admire mountains from a distance since she's a bit afraid of heights. She graduated from Southwest Missouri University and lives in Joplin, Missouri, near her children and five grandchildren. She hopes her grandchildren will love her books as much as she has loved writing them, once they learn to read.